Paper Bullets

Paper Bullets

Lighter Poems by Julie Kane

White Violet Press

ISBN: 13: 978-0615879031

Cover art: Judy M Johnson, *www.papergoodies.com*
Restored 1950 Merrill Paper Doll #3449

White Violet Press
24600 Mountain Avenue, 35
Hemet, California 92544

This one's for you, Dad

—Edwin Julian Kane (1924-2000)

Acknowledgments

Grateful thanks to the editors of the following publications in which the listed poems appeared, sometimes in a slightly different form:

Lighten Up Online: "Bad Boys," "The Best Defense," "The Cat Lady Gets a Dog," "Caveat," "Post-Feminism," "Status Update," and "The California Condor" (as "Urohydrosis").
Light Quarterly: "Bummer," "Lifestyles of the Rich and Famous," "Location, Location," "Looker," "Middle-Aged Woman as Directional Aid," "New Cute Guy," "Plea Bargain," "Turbulence," and "Water Pressure."
Los Angeles Times: "Déjà Vu in the Homeland."
The Mayo Review: "Emily, Walt, and Edna Rewrite 'Heartbreak Hotel.'"
The McNeese Review: "Five Things I Hate That Other People Seem to Love."
Mezzo Cammin: "After Your Hysterectomy."
Poemeleon: "Wrong Things They Taught Me" (as "Learning Curve").
Poetry: A Pocket Anthology, Ed. R. S. Gwynn (Penguin, 2013): "Alan Doll Rap."
Prairie Schooner: "Morning Sex" and "The Ballade of Hirsuteness of Yore."
The Rotary Dial: "Toast."
So It Goes: The Literary Journal of the Kurt Vonnegut Memorial Library: "One Veteran's Tale."
Southern Women's Review: "Men Who Love Redheads."
The Spectator: "Hiawatha Joins Facebook" (a winner of Competition #2653).
Umbrella/Bumbershoot: "Diva," "Unplanned Obsolescence," and "Wallace Stevens Suite."

One of the poems in the sequence "Emily, Walt, and Edna Rewrite 'Heartbreak Hotel'" received an honorable mention in *The Spectator's* Competition #2570.

"Alan Doll Rap" was reprinted in *Literature: A Pocket Anthology*, Ed. R. S. Gwynn (Penguin, 2013), and in *Inside Literature: Reading, Responding, and Arguing,* Ed. R. S. Gwynn and Steven J. Zani (Penguin, 2006).

"Plea Bargain" was reprinted in *The Iron Book of New Humorous Verse,* Ed. Eileen Jones (Iron Press, 2010).

"Status Update" was reprinted in *All Said & Done,* Ed. David Sollis (Tap Poetry, 2012).

Table of Contents

The War with Time

"Shall quips and sentences and these paper bullets of the brain awe a man from the career of his humour?"

—Shakespeare, *Much Ado About Nothing* (Act II, Scene 3)

Gender Wars

New Cute Guy

Not sure yet
If he's straight or gay?
I'll just bet
He feels the same way.

Don't Fall for a Poet Who's Scottish

Don't fall for a poet who's Scottish,
No matter how tallish and hottish.
He'll promise to write,
Then drop out of sight,
Though you liked him an awfully lottish.

Status Update

On Facebook, for "RELATIONSHIP,"
You check the box for mated.
Then he signs up as single and
Oh, crap!—you should have waited.

As soon as his computer's down
Or he's inebriated,
You'll update hoping he won't see
You're now "IT'S COMPLICATED."

Bad Boys

Good boys are bad, and bad boys good,
At making out and dancing slow.
That's why all girls, in maidenhood,
prefer the latter kind of beau.

Men Who Love Redheads

You can pick one out in a crowd
by the way he jerks his head
when an Irish setter passes,
drawn to that shade of red;
or the pickup line he utters
even to Raggedy Ann:
"If all your freckles merged,
do you know you'd have a tan?"

There are times you miss the clues
till you wake up after sex
to behold the nightstand photo
of his red-haired kids and ex;
then you know, for all of your charms,
he was only caught in the pull
of that least-known force of physics,
as a red flag draws a bull.

Some obsessives like girls plump
or missing a limb or two,
but the men hung up on redheads
are the men who prey on you.
Compared to men as a whole,
their numbers are very small,
yet without their kind in the world
you might never get laid at all.

Alan Doll Rap

When I was ten
I wanted a Ken
to marry Barbie
I was into patriarchy
for plastic dolls
eleven inches tall
cuz the sixties hadn't yet
happened at all
Those demonstrations
assassinations
conflagrations across the nation
still nothin but a speck in the imagination
Yeah, Ken was the man
but my mama had the cash
and the boy doll she bought me
was ersatz
"Alan" was his name
from the discount store
He cost a dollar ninety-nine
Ken was two dollars more
Alan's hair was felt
stuck on with cheap glue
like the top of a pool table
scuffed up by cues
and it fell out in patches
when he was brand new
Ken's hair was plastic
molded in waves
coated with paint
no Ken bad-hair days
Well they wore the same size
they wore the same clothes

but Ken was a player
and Alan was a boze
Barbie looked around
at all the other Barbies
drivin up in Dream Cars
at the Ken-and-Barbie party
and knew life had dealt her
a jack, not a king
knew if Alan bought her
an engagement ring
it wouldn't scratch glass
bet your ass
no class
made of cubic zirconia
or cubic Plexiglas
Kens would move Barbies
out of their townhouses
into their dream-houses
Pepto-Bismol pink
from the rugs to the sink
wrap her in mink
but Alan was a bum
Our doll was not dumb
She knew a fronter from a chum
Take off that tuxedo
Alan would torpedo
for the Barcalounger
Bye-bye libido
Hello VCR
No job, no car
Drinkin up her home bar

Stinkin up her boudoir with his cigar
Shrinkin up the cash advance
on her MasterCard
and tryin on her pink peignoir
Till she'd be saying:
"Where's that giant hand
used to make him *stand,*
used to make him *walk?*"

Canon Wars

Wallace Stevens Suite

Funday Morning

A lady skips church on a Sunday,
deciding she'll just have a fun day.
Good riddance, Almighty!
She loafs in her nightie.
Some pigeons swoop low. Then it's Monday.

The Emperor of Ice Cream's New Clothes

One has to look up half the words:
"ice cream" is "concupiscent curds."
A dead lady's feet
stick out from a sheet.
Cigar smoke wafts up to the birds.

Anecdote of a Litterbug

Amidst all that Tennessee beauty,
I did something rather pollute-y.
I ditched, on a mound,
a jar gray and round.
The litter police were off duty.

Hiawatha Joins Facebook

Glitchy software made him gloomy,
But his mission lay before him:
At an antiquated laptop,
On a modem that was dial-up,
To defeat the website filter
That his granny had installed there;
To mark "login" box, then "password"
Like the pale bark of the birch-tree
With his art of picture-writing,
So his friend request could reach her—
Minnie H. from North Dakota,
Savvy owner of an iPad,
She with callused thumbs from texting.
Would she add him or ignore him?
He clicked "like" for Redskins fan page
As his granny lay there snoring . . .

Emily, Walt, and Edna Rewrite "Heartbreak Hotel"

Emily

'Tis down a Street—called Lonely—
That Guest House—where I dwell—
The Bell Hops' Tears—keep flowing—
The Guests—have Tales to tell.

Eons—since Baby left me—
To Desk Clerks—garbed in Black—
And I surmised—the Lodgers' Eyes
Weren't ever looking back.

Walt

I saw at the end of Lonely Street, with tear-filled orbs I mark'd it,
Saw the mournful hotel call'd Heartbreak, the lodge of the
    forsaken,
And I knew that, though it contain'd multitudes, I could always
    find a room there,
And I knew that it was a dwelling-place for broken-hearted lovers,
The bellhops weeping and moaning, and I longing to comfort
    them,
The desk clerks keening in black, and I longing to ease their
    sorrows,
To part the jet cloth from their bosom-bones and thrust my rude
    tongue athwart them.

Edna

I shan't be checking into that hotel,
Although some say there is a vacancy:
The somber occupants have tales to tell
And fain would blame their broken hearts on me.
Awake I've lain in every numbered room
Beside a husband of a single night
Who can do naught but weep away his gloom
Midst clerks in garments coloured anthracite.
Ask not why death forsakes this mournful inn
Whose lodgers grieve for my ephemeral charms,
Nor why I jilted them to lie in sin
Each weeknight in a diff'rent pair of arms:
Believe that ardour drew me to each man,
But Baby's got a short attention span.

The Lost Fascicle

128

Bring me the sunset in a cup—
And a Tequila Sunrise, while you're up.

129

Cocoon above! Cocoon below!
I hate to dust, as well you know.

132

I bring an unaccustomed wine:
Rotgut, a dollar ninety-nine.

204

A slash of Blue—
A sweep of Gray—
Paul Newman still
Grabs me that way.

213

Did the Harebell lose her girdle
To the lover Bee?
That is one Soft-Porn Flick
I don't care to see.

241

I like a look of Agony,
Because I know it's true—
If you're a masochistic Gent,
I'd like to Paddle you.

263

A single Screw of Flesh
Can certainly refresh!

273

He put the Belt around my life—
I heard the Buckle snap—
And turned away, Imperial,
From my Daytona lap.

304

The Day came slow—till Five o'clock—
At last—A Bourbon on the Rocks.

317

Just so—Jesus—raps—
He—doesn't weary—
Eminem and Jay-Z
Are understandably leery.

333

The Grass so little has to do—
If you're watching it, that makes two.

341

After great pain, a formal feeling comes—
The Nerves sit ceremonious, like Tombs—
If your Physician gives you Percoset,
An altogether different High from 'Shrooms.

419

We grow accustomed to the Dark—
When Light is put away—
But when the Light's out in the Fridge
We grope for Chardonnay.

441

This is my letter to the World
That never wrote to Me—
There was no Email—way back then—
Or Spam—as you can see.

465

I heard a Fly buzz—when I died—
The swatter had been left outside.

470

I am alive—I guess—
If not: S.O.S.!

485

To make One's Toilette—after Death
Has made the Toilette cool—
It's best to warm the Toilette up
When used as Swimming Pool.

525

I think the Hemlock likes to stand
Upon a Marge of Snow.
They don't like to be stood upon,
The Marges that I know.

712

Because I could not stop for Death—
He kindly stopped for me—
The Harley should have tipped me off,
And the Hells Angels tee.

754

My Life had stood—a Loaded Gun—
In Corners—till a Day
I had the Sense to empty it
And put the Shells away.

818

I could not drink it, Sweet,
Till you had tasted first—
You might be out to poison me.
I always fear the worst.

878

The Sun is gay or stark—
Gay as Hell when it's dark!

1022

I knew that I had gained
And yet I knew not how:
Perhaps that pint of Haagen-Dazs
Was not Weight Watchers chow?

1052

I never saw a Moor—
I never saw the Sea—
I traveled all around the World
But texted constantly.

1149

I noticed People disappeared
When but a little child—
Perhaps because I kicked their Shins?
I was a little wild.

1154

A full fed Rose on meals of Tint
A Dinner for a Bee—
But if you're picking up the Tab
It's Caviar for me.

1215

I bet with every Wind that blew.
I'm in G.A. now, on Step Two.

1450

The Road was lit with Moon and Star
And High Beams from some Asshole's Car.

1555

I groped for him before I knew
That he had but one Ball, not two.

1590

Not at Home to Callers
Says the Naked Tree—
Gentlemen, come calling!
Says the Naked Me.

1598

Who is it seeks my Pillow Nights?
A Cat who poops but never wipes.

1739

Some say goodnight—at night—
I say goodnight by day—
I say goodbye to mean hello—
I'm weird as hell that way.

Man vs. Nature vs. Nature

The California Condor

The California condor
Takes steps to beat the heat
With methods odd to ponder:
By peeing on its feet.

Evaporating water
Then cools those scaly toes.
Around them, when it's hotter,
It's best to pinch one's nose.

Protective Coloration

The viceroy is delicious
To birds who seek a snack,
Unlike its twin, the monarch,
Who really tastes like crap.

A bird who eats a monarch
Won't make that error twice:
That's why the mon's appearance
Is mimicked by the vice.

So we are taught as children.
But me, I fear the worst:
What if a hungry robin
Devours a viceroy first?

Turbulence

Clouds are pretty up above
but shitty in the middle of.

The Cat Lady Gets a Dog

They worship you, obey you, do tricks for you,
Even let you put sweaters and hats on them!
Best of all is you start getting greeting cards
Without all those frigging cats on them.

;lues

                    :el disgusted
                 stress lyin' in the street
Nc   .og feels disgusted
With h.. mistress lyin' in the street

One tug of my leash, and that woman done lost her feet

Tell me, what are those white things
Scattered all around her face
Could be chips off a milkbone
Scattered all around her face

Well they sure look delicious, I think I'll have a taste

She can moan like a coonhound
With that her arm gripped to her side
Loud and low as a coonhound
With that arm gripped to her side

It may be a long time before she takes me for a ride

And now here comes the mailman
Askin' can he help her up
Well I sure hate that mailman
Askin' can he help her up

One nip of his pants, and he'll learn not to mess with this pup

Skirmishes

Bummer

"Hey, Dad—you got a cigarette?"
I'd ask when young and broke.
"Don't worry about me, my pet!"
He'd say (and have a smoke).

One Veteran's Tale

"Did you kill anybody in the war, Dad?"
(We grab stuffed bears, and cling.)
"Not only did I never *fire* my gun,
I never *cleaned* the thing."

Water Pressure

My neighbor can't water his lawn when I shower,
And I cannot bathe when he sprays.
When he gets a yen to start soaking his flowers,
My armpits might smell bad for days.

I've gone to the Mayor, but this is the South;
The workmen would rather not sweat.
They're deaf to complaints from a feminine mouth,
And no one's been bribed for it yet.

One time I was coated in soap like a lamb
In ringlets of woolly white hair
When all of a sudden the water, goddamn,
Cut off with me sudsy and bare.

I threw on a towel, I ran out the door—
Let's hope that it covered my crotch.
I meant to ask nicely for five minutes more
But set off our Neighborhood Watch.

Five Things I Hate That Other People Seem to Love

1. Melted Orange Cheese

I can't get into melted orange cheese
Poured over plates of fries or nacho chips.
The very notion gives me the dry heaves:
Coagulating clumps of goopy cheese
The color of the thread in dungarees.
I "just say no" to quesadilla dip.
Oh, tablemates, don't order melted cheese
Poured over plates of fries or nacho chips.

2. The Smell of Gasoline

So many folks breathe in while pumping gas
As if they'd caught a whiff of Eau de Joy.
I wonder if they must be stoned on grass.
I'd rather smell a rhino passing gas
Or incense stinking up a Latin mass.
At luaus, they're the ones who love the poi.
So many folks breathe in while pumping gas
As if they'd caught a whiff of Eau de Joy.

3. Sushi

I hate it when my friends go out for sushi
And I get stuck again with teriyaki.
The sushi chefs look fierce as John Belushi
Waving kamikaze swords at sushi,

And sushi-breath can really ruin smoochies
Unless you gargle with a lot of saki.
I hate it when my friends go out for sushi
And I get stuck again with teriyaki.

4. Alcohol

The problem is I loved it too damn much
And now I can't have any more at all.
At thirty-seven I was quite the lush.
The problem is I loved it too damn much.
Don't think I'm Carrie Nation, apt to flush
Your bourbon down the nearest toilet stall.
The problem is I loved it too damn much
And now I can't have any more at all.

5. (A Year Ago I Would Have Listed Dogs)

A year ago I would have listed dogs.
I liked my up-to-that-point dogless life.
Bad breath, crotch sniffing, muddy little paws:
A year ago I would have listed dogs,
But since that time I've softened up because
One shelter photo stabbed me like a knife.
I can't help thinking, being wrong on dogs,
About my husbandless and childless life.

The Rivals

There were only three contenders
For the great big poetry prize—
Two of the feminine gender,
My frenemy and I.
So we went to lunch, extenders
Of the peace pipe, civilized.

"You are so much more deserving,"
She said, "than little old me."
"I'm not fit to be your servant,"
I said, "at poetry."
Yet we both remained observant
For toxins slipped in our tea.

"If not this year, then later,"
My frenemy said then.
I said, "Once nominated,
It's only a matter of when."
But a lot can happen, waiting.
And how long—two years? Ten?

"But you know—I'm ten years older,"
She let slip over dessert.
"I've had *melanoma!*" I told her.
"*My* death is sure to come first!"
Then the room grew suddenly colder
And the versifiers, terse.

Toast

Here's to our friend from work,
Promoted to a jerk.

The War on Ignorance

The Best Defense

The day I handed essays back,
I faced her blazing eyes:
"You're wrong about me, Dr. Kane:
I didn't plagiarize!"

"But it was copied word for word."
"I can explain!" she pleaded.
"I gave it to my friend to write,
And *she's* the one who cheated."

After Dylan Thomas

O lovers groping in the far back row:
I write for you, it's true. But teach? Hell, no!

Excuses, Excuses

A death in the family,
A bout with the flu,
A friend with a flat
Who's depending on you:

Believable boyfriend
(Your voice a caress),
If you were my student,
I'd smell the b.s.

Post-Feminism

If male professors called a female "girl"
Back then, we *women* in the class would hiss.

These days, if anybody calls me that,
I want to give the guy a big fat kiss.

Déjà Vu in the Homeland

"Better dead than red."
—Cold War saying

In school we were taught that a Red
Was a person one really should dread:
For they spied on one's mail,
Locked the untried in jail—
Now I guess we'd be better off dead.

Wrong Things They Taught Me

—For Urie Bronfenbrenner (1917-2005)

Mother

To brush one's hair a hundred strokes a night
To fry a burger in a pan of salt
That tampons robbed one of virginity
To always let the boy be first to call
To give a child an aspirin for sore throat
To wash white gloves out nightly in the sink
That gold and silver clashed, and brown and black
That broccoli was best when steamed till limp

Teachers

That Russia was our greatest enemy
That cowboys were the good guys, Injuns bad
To kneel down with one's arms above one's head
Below the desk in an atomic blast
Two hundred million in the U.S.A.
Three billion on the surface of the globe
That French was spoken by all diplomats
(Though Esperanto was the future's hope)

Nuns

That girls not named for saints would go to hell
That newborn infants had already sinned
To never enter church without a hat
(Though squares of Kleenex could be bobby-pinned)
To fast all night before one took the host
To stick one's *tongue* out for it, not the hands
That patent leather shoes reflected all
And boys would peek to see one's underpants

Friends

To wear white lipstick for the "London Look"
To rat one's hair to make it pouf on top
That baby oil would give the perfect tan
That incense covered up the smell of pot
To not trust anybody 31
To save one's calories for alcohol
That bras were only good to toss in flames
(Though Newton figured out that apples fall)

Professors

That schizophrenics had their moms to blame
That stomach ulcers were brought on by stress
That female animals would always fall
For males whose plumage was the showiest
To make a carbon copy when one types
That women climax from the womb, not clit
That authors' bios were irrelevant
To understanding works of western lit

Coda

But one man taught me how to live in doubt,
The only teaching I have not thrown out.

Caveat

Oh, stay on your toes around those who write prose,
For they'll rob you of every good story.
Without much repentance, they'll steal every sentence
You utter, to further their glory.

What you said about sex, all the dirt on your ex,
Your confessions re crime or addiction—
When you share all the poop with your therapy group,
They'll remark how your life mimics fiction.

Be especially cool around MFA schools,
Where they're all wearing wires like informers;
Be as dull as a shrub when you chat in the pub,
Or they'll market the film rights to Warner's.

You can let down your guard when you're next to a bard,
For they rarely get out of their psyches,
Being so self-absorbed, as you gaze in their orbs,
They don't notice you're nude in your Nikes.

But beware of that kind whose right margins are lined,
And stay mum when they sit at your table;
They can steal your good name or your purse, all the same,
But who steals your life's plot, steals your navel.

Diva

If I could sing, I wouldn't write this shit
for intellectuals who read too much:
I'd be a diva, you can bet on it,

adored by teenybopper fans with zits,
adorning magazines from *Elle* to *Us*.
If I could sing, I wouldn't write this shit.

Oh, Justin Timberlake would bare my tit
on MTV in an attack of lust.
I'd be a diva, you can bet on it.

I might OD, but I would never slit
my wrists or turn the gas up, more robust
than pallid poets churning out this shit.

The moving finger writes and, having writ,
shoots bards a middle digit pointing up
while divas count the moola from their hits.

Ask Whitney, Britney, jitneys full of Brits
from sixties pop invasions—writing sucks!
Ask Lady Gaga, Cher, or Stevie Nicks.
They'd all stay divas, you can bet on it.

The War with Time

Middle-Aged Woman as Directional Aid

"Cows automatically point to the north because they have their own in-built compasses aligning them with the Earth's magnetic field, scientists have discovered."
—*The Telegraph,* 26 Aug 2008

The news is out that cows are pointing north:
I guess they mean the end that has a mouth,
Because the other end, like me these days,
Has udders that are always pointing south.

Lifestyles of the Rich and Famous

I get my house cleaned once a week,
I get my hair done twice.
A host of chefs bring fine cuisine,
My taste buds to entice.

I must have married rich, you guess,
On figure, looks, and charm.
The truth is much less glamorous:
I fell and broke my arm.

Looker

This morning in the grocery store
I felt the bag-boys stare
The way men used to stare at me,
Down to my underwear.

Was it the seven pounds I'd lost?
I struck a sexy pose.
When I got home, the mirror showed
A black smudge on my nose.

Morning Sex

Pre-Viagra, pre-Cialis,
When my beaux were young and randy,
Always poking with a phallus,
It was just a snack, like candy.

How I miss those long-bygone days
When the flesh was firm and fecund:
Now the snack's become the entrée,
And there's not a hope of seconds.

The Ballade of Hirsuteness of Yore

Where, pray tell, in what sewer drain
Reposes that pectoral rug
That seemed to the young Julie Kane
Such a poppy-field-like drug
When she'd nestle her hairless mug
On a boyfriend's chest? Razors, Nair—
Be damned! Calvin Klein models—ugh!
Where are the shows of frontal hair?

Where did Catholic high-school swains
With the holy medals she dug
(Hypnotic on silk cord or chain
Over chest fur and swimming trunks)
Go? Younger women just shrug;
They don't understand her despair,
Out of date as the jitterbug.
Where are the shows of frontal hair?

Yet those same old boyfriends might faint
To see how *she* has been plucked
Since the days when they'd tell her, "It's plain
You're a natural redhead, my love."
These days it's "Brazilian," one tuft
In a fanciful shape, down there,
In place of that seventies shrub.
Where are the rows of pubic hair?

Black, curly vee in Casey's scrubs,
In Playboy crotch-shot: gone, but where?
When did we all go smooth as slugs?
Where are the shows of frontal hair?

After Your Hysterectomy

You cannot get your stomach wet:
Damp towel dab it.

You cannot drive a car just yet:
You'll have to cab it.

You cannot lift a thing with heft:
So do not grab it.

You cannot smoke a cigarette:
So kick that habit.

And if only you'd been having sex
You couldn't have it.

Location, Location

"So very convenient!" she says of my plot,
My elderly South Asian friend.

The graveyard is right at the end of my block,
The street an emphatic dead-end.

For mourners to walk back to food, drink, and talk
Once I (in my pine box) descend?

Or me to go haunting my house, once re-bought?
I'd ask, but don't wish to offend.

Unplanned Obsolescence

I wish I hadn't mentioned pay phone dimes
or female hurricanes, or pink foam rollers.
My poems slowly slip behind the times.
I wish I hadn't mentioned pay phone dimes.
Soon, editors will footnote all my lines
as coffin thieves pry silver from my molars.
I wish I hadn't mentioned pay phone dimes
or female hurricanes, or pink foam rollers.

Plea Bargain

Inside the scanner's tunnel,
you swear that you will be
a candidate for sainthood
if spared from the big C.

You'll help to feed the hungry,
you'll comfort the bereft;
you'll minister to lepers
if there are any left.

But when the doctors tell you
that you are in the pink,
the terms that you agreed to
seem rather harsh, you think:

perhaps another kitten,
a shelter rescue pet,
or pound of fair-trade coffee
would settle up the debt.

Previous Books by Julie Kane

Poetry:

Jazz Funeral (Story Line Press, 2009). Winner of the 2009 Donald Justice Poetry Prize (judged by David Mason).

Rhythm & Booze (University of Illinois Press, 2003). Winner of the 2002 National Poetry Series (selected by Maxine Kumin). Finalist for the 2005 Poets' Prize.

Body and Soul (Pirogue, 1987).

Nonfiction:

With co-author Kiem Do: *Counterpart: A South Vietnamese Naval Officer's War* (Naval Institute Press, 1998). History Book Club Featured Alternate Selection, Spring 1999.

Edited Anthology:

With co-editor Grace Bauer: *Umpteen Ways of Looking at a Possum: Critical and Creative Responses to Everette Maddox* (Xavier Review Press, 2006). Finalist for the 2007 Southern Independent Booksellers Alliance (SIBA) Book Prize in Poetry.

About the Author

A native of Boston and longtime resident of Louisiana, Julie Kane was the 2011-2013 Louisiana Poet Laureate. She teaches at Northwestern State University in Natchitoches. Awards for her poetry include the Donald Justice Poetry Prize, National Poetry Series selection, a Fulbright Scholarship in Creative Writing/American Studies, the Open Poetry International Sonnet Award, an Academy of American Poets Prize, a Glenna Luschei *Prairie Schooner* Poetry Prize, first prize in the *Mademoiselle Magazine* College Poetry Competition, and the George Bennett Fellowship in Writing at Phillips Exeter Academy. She has published several essays on women writers of light verse, and apparently it was contagious.

CPSIA information can be obtained
at www.ICGtesting.com
Printed in the USA
BVHW041138200320
575549BV00012B/157